Writing Prompts for Kids

On Quotes From Historical Figures

Linda Chiara

Ontrakmedia

Book Cover by Ontrakmedia

First edition 2023

Contents

Dear Parents and Educators

Great minds speak not only through their words, but also through their actions. The following quotations, spoken by some of the most influential figures in history, serve as a reminder of the power of inspiration and the wisdom that can be gained from those who have come before us.

As we delve into the world of these famous quotations, we'll come across a diverse range of perspectives and ideas, from the powerful and transformative words of Martin Luther King Jr. to the wise and timeless sayings of Confucius. Your students will be exposed to a wealth of knowledge and insight.

I'll explain each quotation in detail and how they relate to your students' own personal experiences. Each quotation will include a writing prompt that will help them easily apply the wisdom of these famous individuals to their own lives and reality.

With these carefully selected and well-developed writing prompts, I intend to amuse, entertain, inspire, and challenge your students' young and developing minds. The prompts should motivate them to pour their passion, thoughts and values into their writing, and help them frame their opinions.

Positive reviews from wonderful readers like you help other parents feel confident about choosing the *Writing Prompts for School Kids on Quotes from Historical Figures* book. Sharing your experience will be greatly appreciated!

I hope you enjoy these writing prompts!

Linda Chiara

One

Writing Prompts on U.S. Presidential Quotes

A president should inspire others and lead by example. Their leadership should motivate people to move forward to make changes for the better no matter how difficult the challenges are. These writing prompts on quotes from presidents will encourage your upper elementary, middle school and high school students to reflect and express their values and opinions.

> 1: *The harder the conflict, the greater the triumph.* (George Washington)
> Why is that true? Wouldn't life be easier if our choices were easy ones? Have you ever faced a truly difficult conflict that you ended up handling well? Write about that experience and explain why what Washington said was true.

2: *On matters of style, swim with the current, on matters of principle, stand like a rock.*
(Thomas Jefferson)
Can you think of a time when you "stood like a rock" on a matter of principle? Were you proud that you held your ground for what you thought was right? Write about that experience.

3: *Try and fail, but don't fail to try.*
(John Quincy Adams)
Do you ever wish you could just give up on something? Have you ever persevered even when it was difficult to do so? Write about a time that you almost felt defeated, but decided to push through and succeed at your task. For example, you can write about the first time you ever tried to cook a meal or your first attempt at bike riding or skiing,

4: *It's easier to do a job right, than to explain why you didn't.*
(Martin Van Buren)
Have you ever completed a task poorly, or maybe didn't even complete it at all and later realized how much easier it would have been to just do it correctly the first time? What consequences were there for not completing the task?

5: *Nearly all men can stand adversity, but if you want to test a man's character, give him power.*
(Abraham Lincoln)
When you suffer through trying times (a family member's illness, loss of friends, loss of home, parents divorcing, etc), you usually end up stronger as a person in the end. But, according to psychologists, the paradox of power is that the very traits that helps someone to become powerful, often disappear once power is achieved. Write about a time when you suffered through adversity and came out stronger in the end. Or you can choose to write about someone who achieved power in your inner circle, who then became difficult to be with as a result.

6: *It's hard to fail, but it is worse never to have tried.*
(Theodore Roosevelt)
Have you ever been afraid to try something new because you feared you would look foolish or not be able to succeed? If you could go back and do it again, would you try the new thing?

7: *Kindness is the only service that will stand the storm of life and not wash out.*
(Abraham Lincoln)
Do you know of someone who makes the world

a better place just by being a kind or thoughtful or caring person? Write about this inspirational person and explain how they teach the truth by living the way they do.

8: *It's amazing what you can accomplish if you do not care who gets the credit.*
(Harry S. Truman)
Have you ever done a team building exercise where you had to work with someone who didn't really do his or her fair share? Is it important for someone's work to be recognized or should just having done a good job overall be enough? Write an essay stating your point of view.

9: *Yesterday is not ours to recover, but tomorrow is ours to win or lose.*
(Lyndon B. Johnson)
When you make a huge mistake, can you let go of it and look toward the future? Or does having done something wrong weigh on you too much? Write an essay about a time you did something for which you feel regret and explain if you were able to let it go or not.

10: *A man is not finished when he's defeated. He's defeated when he quits.*

(Richard M. Nixon)

This is a fancy way of saying, "if at first you don't succeed, try, try again." Have you ever given up on something (a sport or a musical instrument, for example), because it was too hard to do? Do you regret it?

11: *The friend in my adversity I shall always cherish most. I can better trust those who helped to relieve the gloom of my dark hours than those who are so ready to enjoy with me the sunshine of my prosperity.*

(Ulysses S. Grant)

Do you have someone who you consider to be only a fair weather friend? Someone who is always there for you when things are going well, but who won't help you when you need it? Write a letter to this person (as an exercise, not to send!) explaining about a time when you really needed their help and they failed to come through.

12: *Believe you can and you're half way there.*

(Theodore Roosevelt)

Do you agree with that statement? Does all it take for a person to succeed is to have confidence? Write about a time when you did something no one else thought you could.

13: *Change will not come if we wait for some other person or some other time. We are the ones we've been waiting for. We are the change that we seek.*
(Barack Obama)
Do you see things you want to change, but don't know how to go about it? Write about something that you'd like to see done differently and devise a plan on how to achieve that goal.

14: *Failure at some point in your life is inevitable, but giving up is unforgivable.*
(Joe Biden)
If you fail at something and then give up, then it's over. But if you keep trying there is a hope that your wishes and dreams can come true. Write about something that you aspire to do, where you know there will be obstacles in your way that you will have to overcome.

15: *It is far better to be alone, than to be in bad company.*
(George Washington)
Have you ever found yourself in a situation where you would have been better off alone, rather than to be hanging out with the people you were with? Write about a time you were with a group of people where you knew you shouldn't stay. Did you

get caught up in acting like them or were you true to yourself and not do whatever it was they were doing?

16: *Plans are nothing; planning is everything.* (Dwight D. Eisenhower)
Are plans and planning the same thing? What do you think Eisenhower meant when he said that?

17: *If you take no risks, you will suffer no defeats. But if you take no risks, you win no victories.* (Richard M. Nixon)
Write about a time where you took a risk that made you feel victorious.

18: *The ballot is stronger than the bullet.* (Abraham Lincoln)
Is that true in your opinion? Can voting truly make a difference? Write about a time when a particular vote altered your world personally. It can be a presidential vote or a vote that was taken in your local community.

19: *There are many ways of going forward, but only one way of standing still.* (Franklin D. Roosevelt)

Standing still means not making a decision. Have you ever been sorry about a time when you "stood still?"

20: *The only thing we have to fear is fear itself.*
(Franklin D. Roosevelt)
Franklin Roosevelt, who was the President of the United States during the Great Depression, is emphasizing the idea that fear can be debilitating, and that it is important to overcome it in order to achieve one's goals. Have you ever failed to take on a new project or adventure for fear of failing? Explain what happened and what you learned from this experience.

Two

Writing Prompts on Confucius Proverbs

These Confucius proverbs writing prompts are a sure way to get your high school, middle school, and older elementary school students thinking critically. Confucius (551-479 BCE) was a Chinese philosopher who is considered to be one of the most influential individuals in history. His philosophical teachings emphasized personal and governmental morality, kindness and justice. His teachings are called Confucianism and they are the basis of East Asian culture and society.

1: *It does not matter how slowly you go as long as you do not stop.*
Like the fable about the tortoise and the hare, it doesn't matter how long it takes you to get to the finish line, as long as you don't stop the way the hare did. Can you think of a situation where it took you a long time to complete something, but you didn't stop until you finished?

2: *A healthy man wants a thousand things, a sick man wants only one.*
Money, power, or health? What do you choose? Does money or power matter if you don't have your health? Explain your answer.

3: *Our greatest glory is not in never falling, but in rising every time we fall.*
That's a pretty fancy way of saying "never give up." Can you think of a time that you kept failing at something, but you kept trying and trying until you succeeded? Write about it.

4: *Everything has beauty, but not everyone sees it.*
Many people think puppies and kittens are beautiful, while others see the beauty in lizards and sharks. Can you think of something that you think is beautiful that perhaps other people do not?

5: *The journey with a thousand miles begins with one step.*
Some people believe that the journey Confucius spoke of was a physical journey, like traveling from New York to Florida. But it's more likely that he was referring to our journey in life, like learning a new language or learning how to paint. Pick

something you would like to learn and explain what first step you would need to get started.

6: *The man who moves a mountain begins by carrying away small stones.*
People don't really move mountains! However, sometimes they have a big project to complete that feels as difficult as moving a mountain. For example, pretend you had to clean up a very messy bedroom which is full of books, dirty clothes, toys, food wrappers and just plain old trash! How would you start to "move that mountain'? Which "small stones" would you first remove to make cleaning the room easier?

7: *Life is really simple, but we insist on making it complicated.*
Write a short essay on ways that human beings make life complicated. Why do you think we do that?

8: *The superior man thinks always of virtue; the common man thinks of comfort.*
Do you think Confucius meant that we should not be comfortable in life? Or is his quote deeper than that? Explain what you think he meant.

9: *He who speaks without modesty will find it difficult to make his words good.*
What do you think Confucius thought about braggarts when you read this quote? Do you think modesty is important or should you be allowed to boast about your accomplishments?

10: *To be wronged is nothing unless you continue to remember it.*
Have you ever had to forgive someone for something that they'd done to hurt you? If you still feel pain from the betrayal, do you think that someday you will be able to forgive so that the wrong is nothing? If not, why not?

11: *The man who asks a question is a fool for a minute, the man who does not ask is a fool for life.*
Are you sometimes afraid to ask a question because you don't want to appear to be foolish or ignorant? Explain what Confucius meant when he said that by NOT asking the question you can be a fool for life.

12: *Success depends upon previous preparation, and without such preparation there is sure to be failure.*

There are many, many examples of this. If you don't study before a test, you're more likely to fail. If you don't have a speech written out, you may drone on and on. If you don't practice at a sport and do the drills required, you'll probably end up being a mediocre athlete. Can you think of a time when you did not prepare, when you should have? What were the end results?

13: *Before you embark on a journey of revenge, dig two graves.*
Confucius was saying revenge hurts both parties. Do you think that is true? Why or why not?

14: *The man who says he can, and the man who says he can't are both correct.*
Confucius believed in the power of positive thinking and in believing in yourself. Does a saying like this inspire you to never give up?

15: *Your life is what your thoughts make it.*
Everyone has a loop of thoughts running in their heads, both good and bad. If you can learn to control your thoughts, you will be able to control some things about your life. Why do you think it's so hard to get rid of negative thoughts?

16: *Real knowledge is to know the extent of one's ignorance.*
How can understanding the extent of your ignorance be the real knowledge? Give an example.

17: *We have two lives, and the second begins when we realize we only have one.*
How can you live your life so that you don't waste time learning this truth?

18: *If you are the smartest person in the room, then you are in the wrong room.*
Explain why you are in the wrong room, if you are the smartest person in it. Should you not aspire to be the smartest person in the room? Or does it mean you should always aspire to learn more?

19: *I hear and I forget. I see and I remember. I do and I understand.*
Give an example of what Confucius meant when he said this.

Three

Writing Prompts on Ben Franklin Quotes

Benjamin Franklin was an extraordinary man. In addition to being one of America's Founding Fathers, he was a diplomat, an inventor, a writer, publisher and a scientist. When the Second Continental Congress established the United States Post Office, he became the first United States Postmaster General. Let these writing prompts on Ben Franklin Quotes spark your students' imaginations.

1: *A penny saved is a penny earned.*
What does that mean exactly? What can you do if you save a penny?

2: *Never leave that till tomorrow what you can do today.*
Is it really so bad if you don't clean your room on the day you are supposed to? What about not taking your dog for a walk when it's time for him

to go out? What would happen if you didn't do the things you were supposed to do each day and left them for another day?

3: *Early to bed, early to rise, makes a man healthy, wealthy and wise.*
How could going to bed early and then waking up early the next day make someone wise, wealthy or healthy?

4: *One today is worth two tomorrows.*
Usually having two of something is better than having one. So what did Ben Franklin mean about two tomorrows? You might have heard of the old saying a bird in hand is worth two in the bush. Is that the same thing?

5: *A place for everything, everything in its place.*
Why is it important to have a place for everything? Is there anything wrong with putting books in the closet or clothes under your bed?

6: *He that lies down with dogs, shall rise up with fleas.*
Clearly, Franklin didn't mean this literally. Dogs have nothing to do with this saying. What do you

think he was indicating in regards to people and their friends or acquaintances?

7: *Some people die at 25, and aren't buried until 75.* Do you know someone who might fit this description? Someone who stopped learning or living their life to the fullest at a young age? Write about that person.

8: *Don't throw stones at your neighbors, if your own windows are glass.*
You might know this quotation better as *people who live in glass houses shouldn't throw stones.* Since it would be rare for someone to actually live in a glass house, what does the saying mean exactly?

9: *Well done is better than well said.*
Have you ever been guilty of this? Have you ever promised to do something and not followed through with your promise? Write about it and explain what kind of negative impact your failed promise might have had.

10: *By failing to prepare, you are preparing to fail.* This quote doesn't just apply to school work, quizzes and tests! Think about a situation in life that has nothing to do with school and write about how important preparation is.

11: *Three can keep a secret, if two of them are dead.* Clearly, the point of this quotation is that you can never tell someone a secret if you want to ensure it remains a secret. No one likes to have their secrets revealed. Have you ever been told a secret that you promised to keep, only to reveal it to someone else? Did you end up losing a friendship over it?

12: *If a man could have half of his wishes, he would double his trouble.*
If you got everything you wanted, why would that be a bad thing?

13: *Half a truth is often a great lie.*
Have you ever told the truth about something, but left out an important piece of information? For instance, do you think that by not telling "the whole truth" you are in essence, lying? Why or why not?

14: *He that rises late, must trot all day*.
Do you like to hit the snooze button on your alarm to sleep a little extra each day? Do you enjoy the extra sleep more than the feeling of running late for the rest of the day?

15: *An egg today is better than a hen tomorrow.*
The premise of this quote is that it is better to have something substantial now, rather than the potential or the promise of something in the future. However, could you not argue that the opposite is true? Better to sacrifice the substantial item (an egg, for example) and hold out for something that will give you more of what you want (a hen who lays eggs everyday) in the future? Pick a side of this debate and argue your point.

16: *It is easier to prevent bad habits than to break them.*
Write about a bad habit that you have. Explain why you wish you'd never started it because of the difficulty breaking it.

17: *It is the eye of other people that ruin us. If I were blind I would want neither fine clothes, fine houses or fine furniture*.
Do you think this is true? If teenagers never saw

what other people wore, or how they decorated their houses, would the pressure of keeping up disappear?

18: *The worst wheel of the cart makes the most noise.*
This expression is also translated as "the squeaky wheel gets the grease." Is that a good thing or a bad thing? Should you be the squeaky wheel to get what you want or do people who make the most noise come off as annoying? Write about the pros and cons of being the "worst wheel of the cart."

19: *Beware of little expenses. A small leak will sink a great ship.*
Are you the type of person who buys unnecessary or frivolous things because, "it only costs a couple of dollars"? Think about how much you've spent on useless things in the last month and write about something you'd like to save for. How long would it take for you to save up for your special item? Write about how you could motivate yourself to save.

20: *Never ruin an apology with an excuse.*
Can you think of a time when someone gave you

an apology only to be followed by excuses? Write about a situation when you or someone you know could have heeded this advice.

21: *You may delay, but time will not.*
We've all been guilty of procrastinating at some point in our life. Write a story about when procrastinating cost you dearly.

22: *Tell me and I forget. Teach me and I remember. Involve me and I learn.*
We all have different learning styles. Visual, auditory, spatial, etc. Can you think of an example where this quotation has applied to you? Did you ever learn something through direct involvement?

23: *Be slow in choosing a friend, and slower in changing.*
Write an essay with your interpretation of what you believe Franklin really meant with this quote.

Four

Writing Prompts on Contradictory Proverbs

Proverbs are sayings that have been around for a long time, which offer advice or state a general truth. But sometimes proverbs can contradict each other. Here are some examples of contradictory proverbs. Pick a group of proverbs and explain why you believe one over the other. Write out your reasons for why you think the way you do.

Writing Prompt 1: *Opposites attract. - Birds of a feather stick together.*
Can you think of a situation where opposites attracted each other and it worked out? Or do you find that having common interests is better?

Writing Prompt 2: *The love of money is the root of all evil. - Money makes the world go round.*
Which is true? Why?

Writing Prompt 3: *Absence makes the heart grow fonder. - Out of sight, out of mind.*
How can both be true? Use an example to explain.

Writing Prompt 4:- *Clothes make the man. - You cannot judge a book by its cover.*
So which is it? Are clothes important to make a good impression to you? Or do you rather not judge a person until you know them better no matter how they appear?

Writing Prompt 5:- *The early bird gets the worm. - Haste makes waste.*
Should you hurry up to get what you're after or do you think that by rushing sometimes people make costly mistakes and lose out on what they were after in the first place?

Five

Writing Prompts on Mark Twain Quotes

These entertaining writing prompts on Mark Twain quotes are guaranteed to get your students engaged. Mark Twain was not only one of the greatest and most influential American writers, but also a celebrated humorist known for his sharp wit and amusing observations. Watch how quickly your students get energized and inspired with these prompts on Mark Twain quotes.

1: *It is better to keep your mouth closed and let people think you are a fool than to open it and remove all doubt.*
Was there ever a time when you opened your mouth and said something that you shouldn't have? Looking back on it now, do you feel foolish for having said it?

2: *If it's your job to eat a frog, it's best to do it first thing in the morning. And If it's your job to eat two frogs, it's best to eat the biggest one first.*
Obviously, eating a frog is a metaphor in Twain's quote. But what do you think his point is in this saying? Can you give an example of when it's better to "eat the biggest frog first" or at least "eat it the first thing in the morning?"

3: *If you tell the truth, you don't have to remember anything.*
Did you ever tell a story that wasn't totally true so many times that you practically convinced yourself that the way you told it is how it really happened? When you think of it now, does the truth of what happened seem a little blurry? Write about the incident.

4: *The best way to cheer yourself up is to try to cheer somebody else up.*
Write about a time when you were feeling sad and you cheered someone else up. What did you do to make them happy? Did your good deed make you forget your own troubles for a while?

5: *It usually takes me more than three weeks to prepare a good impromptu speech.*

What does Mark Twain suggest about being prepared in this quote? Can you think of something that you do where you prepare so much that when you do the task, you make it look easy?

6: *The secret of getting ahead is getting started.*
Do you procrastinate? Have you ever procrastinated on a homework assignment or studying for a test, only to realize that once you did get started, it wasn't as difficult as you had feared? Write about it.

7: *It's not the size of the dog in the fight, it's the size of the fight in the dog.*
Mark Twain is not talking about an actual dog fight in this quote. He is alluding to our confidence level. Give an example of a time where you "won a fight" because you were confident in what you were doing or saying.

8: *A full belly is little worth where the mind is starved.*
Are all the riches of the world a good substitute for ignorance? Write an essay on your point of view.

9: *A man cannot be comfortable without his own approval.*
What do you think Mark Twain meant by this?

10: *Travel is fatal to prejudice.*
It is often said that traveling makes you a more open-minded person. Traveling produces en-counters between strangers and exposes you to new cultures. It's conducive to experiences you would have otherwise not had. Write an essay about how traveling could enrich your life.

11: *Honor is a harder master than law.*
Can you be dishonorable even though you've nev-er broken the law? Write an example.

12: *A lie can travel halfway around the world while the truth is putting on its shoes.*
Why do you think it is that lies, or rumors, spread so quickly? Why does it take so long for the truth to come out after a damaging lie and be accepted as the truth?

Six

Writing Prompts on Mahatma Gandhi Quotes

Mahatma Gandhi was one of the most important political and spiritual leaders of the 20th century. He was a key figure in the Indian independence movement and is widely regarded as the father of the nation. He inspired movements for civil rights and freedom across the world through his philosophy of non-violent civil disobedience. His quotes continues to inspire millions of people all over the world, as they are simple yet powerful, with a universal appeal. Use these quotes to relate how they may apply to your own personal life.

1: *The difference between what we do and what we are capable of doing would suffice to solve most of the world's problems.*
Gandhi's quote is a reminder that each person has the power to make a difference, and that the

small efforts of many can add up to make a big impact. Think of a world problem you'd like to find a solution to, and write about the type of small acts that can contribute to its solution.

2: *The weak can never forgive. Forgiveness is the attribute of the strong.*
Do you believe that it takes a strong person to be able to forgive someone who has wronged them? Explain your thoughts.

3: *An eye for an eye will only make the world blind.*
If we all seek retaliation and revenge on those who have wronged us, it will only lead to a cycle of violence and ultimately everyone will be harmed. Why do you agree or disagree with this statement?

4: *Strength does not come from physical capacity. It comes from an indomitable will.*
Gandhi believed that an indomitable will, or a strong determination, is what allows a person to overcome obstacles and achieve their goals. Can you think of some examples where mental strength is needed over physical strength?

5: *The true measure of any society can be found in how it treats its most vulnerable members.*
Should a society protect and care for those who are vulnerable and marginalized? If you were in charge of a big city, how would you achieve this?

6: *You must be the change you wish to see in the world.*
This is one of Gandhi's most famous quotes and it speaks to the idea that in order to bring about change in the world, we must first change ourselves. What advice would you give today your younger self?

7: *First they ignore you, then they laugh at you, then they fight you, then you win.*
Though this quote is often attributed to Gandhi, it's not clear if it was a direct quote. In any case, when someone is advocating for change, they will often be ignored or dismissed at first, but if they persist they will eventually be taken seriously and their message will be heard. Has this ever happened to you? Write about it.

8: *Poverty is the worst form of violence.*
Should it not be the duty of society to eradicate

poverty? What would you propose to solve the problem of poverty worldwide?

9: *Happiness is when what you think, what you say, and what you do are in harmony.*
Do you believe that it is true that when your actions, words, and thoughts are all aligned and consistent with one another? Another way to say it, is if you want to lead a fulfilling life don't pretend you're someone other than who you are. Write a story of someone, real or fictitious, who you believe has not heeded this advice.

10. *The best way to find yourself is to lose yourself in the service of others.* When you serve others, you gain a deeper understanding of yourself and your own values and purpose in life. Write an essay explaining how you are able to achieve personal growth through some specific volunteer work you carry out in your own community. Use an example.

Seven

Writing Prompts on Shakespeare Quotes

Shakespeare is considered one of the greatest writers in the English language and his influence on literature, theater, and culture is incalculable. His works have been translated into every major language and continue to be studied and performed around the world. These quotes explore the universal themes of love, jealousy, ambition, and betrayal. They may serve as a great inspiration for writing prompts particularly at the **high school level.**

1: *All the world's a stage, and all the men and women merely players.*
(As You Like It.)
Life is like a play and we are all performing different parts. If you could choose your role in life what would it be? Would you be the empathetic listener, the bully, the nosey neighbor next door, the betrayed lover, the comic? Pick any role you'd like and write a story about yourself.

2: *All that glitters is not gold.*
(The Merchant of Venice.)
Things that look valuable or attractive at the surface may not be as valuable as they seem. Who hasn't been let down or disappointed before? Maybe it was something you purchased or maybe it was someone you met. Write a story about your disappointment and what you learned from it.

3: *Cowards die many times before their deaths; The valiant never taste of death but once.*
(Julius Cesar)
A brave person dies only once; the coward has to live with his cowardliness for his entire life and dies of fear or shame many times before his actual death. Thinking at a personal level, have you ever done something where you've been cowardly about it, and then found that you had to live with the consequences? Write a story about it and the lessons you learned from it.

4: *To err is human; to forgive, divine.*
(All's Well That Ends Well)
Forgiveness is truly a virtue. It's important to be able to forgive others if we wish to be forgiven ourselves. Write an essay about a time when someone made a mistake and you had to forgive

them, or a time when you erred and had to be forgiven.

5: *Love all, trust a few, do wrong to none.*
(All's Well That Ends Well)
Explain in your words the pros and the cons of opening your heart to everyone regardless of whether they have your best interest at heart, while putting your trust in only a few, and doing no one wrong.

6: *What's in a name? That which we call a rose by any other name would smell as sweet.*
(Romeo and Juliet)
Think of a food you really love, like chocolate or pizza. If it were called "Slimy Guts" would it still be as palatable to you? Or would you reject it because of its name? How do you feel about it?

7: *A fool thinks of himself to be wise, but a wise man knows himself to be a fool,*
(As You Like It)
What do you believe Shakespeare meant with this quote? Write your opinion.

Eight

Writing Prompts on Winston Churchill Quotes

These quotes reflect Churchill's strong leadership style, his unwavering determination, and his profound understanding of human nature. He is widely considered as one of the greatest wartime leaders of the 20th century and his quotes evolve around the topic of courage and fierce determination. Use the wisdom of Churchill's quotes to stimulate and inspire even your most reluctant student writers.

1: *Courage is what it takes to stand up and speak; courage is also what it takes to sit down and listen.* The quote is a reminder that in any conversation, both speaking and listening are important and both often require courage. It's a call to be open-minded, to listen and to consider other people's opinions and perspectives. Write a story about a time you put aside your own biases and opinions, and respectfully listened to an opposing view that ultimately helped you change your mind.

2: *Success is not how high you have climbed, but how you make a positive difference to the world.*
A person's true success is not measured by one's personal achievements or status, but by the impact they have on others and the community and world around them. How do YOU measure success? Whether in sports, school band, the debate club or any other school activity, are you willing to forego personal recognition in the spirit of team success? Write about a time you did just that.

3: *It is a mistake to look too far ahead. Only one link of the chain of destiny can be handled at a time.*
While it's important to focus on future goals and outcomes, don't you need to focus also on the present and take things one step at a time? Or do you believe that without focusing on your future plans, you'll waste opportunities that could help you meet your long-term goals? What is your opinion on this?

4: *You have enemies? Good. That means you've stood up for something, sometime in your life.*

Is it possible to go through life without making any enemies or generating any sort of animosity from others towards yourself? What is your opinion?

5: *The greatest lesson in life is to know that even fools are right sometimes.*

It's not uncommon for us to automatically dismiss the ideas and thoughts of someone whom we dislike or for whom we don't have a great deal of personal respect. However, should we be humble enough to accept that sometimes those same individuals may be right about something and prove us wrong? Write about a time when someone with whom you normally wouldn't agree on anything, was able to change your mind.

Nine

Writing Prompts on Martin Luther King Quotes

Martin Luther King, Jr. (1929-1968) was a Baptist minister and civil rights activist who played a key role in the American civil rights movement from the mid-1950s until his assassination in 1968. He is best known for his role in the advancement of civil rights using nonviolent civil disobedience based on his Christian beliefs. His quotations typically reflect, and are a symbol of, the struggle for civil rights and racial equality to which he dedicated his life.

1: *Injustice anywhere is a threat to justice every-where.*
It is important to stand up against injustice and fight for equality, not just for oneself but for oth-ers as well. Dr. King was advocating that the fight for Civil Rights was not just a fight for the African American community, but a fight for the rights

and dignity of all people. Have you ever stood up and took action against what you felt was an injustice? Write about the circumstances in which you did and the subsequent outcome.

2: *Faith is taking the first step even when you don't see the whole staircase.*
Dr. King was a man of deep faith, and this quote reflects his belief that through faith and determination, one can overcome even the most daunting obstacles. But this is a quote that can be applied in many aspects of life, from your personal to your school life and career aspirations. Write an essay that demonstrates how you apply the meaning of this quotation in your own life.

3. *The ultimate measure of a man is not where he stands in moments of comfort and convenience, but where he stands at times of challenge and controversy.*
Have you ever taken a stand that was uncomfortable and controversial? Did you back down too get back to a place of comfort or did you hold steady in your convictions and not give in to pressure. Write about it.

4. Change does not roll in on the wheels of inevitability, but comes through continuous struggle. And so we must straighten our backs and work for our freedom. A man can't ride you unless your back is bent. Change and progress require active participation and hard work; true freedom cannot be attained without effort and struggle. The act of keeping yourself upright and standing tall - physically and metaphorically - is a symbol of resistance to oppression. Write a story of someone who stood up for their principles. You can choose either someone you personally know or a historical figure.

Ten

Writing Prompts on Dr. Seuss Quotes

Dr. Seuss was a prolific writer whose children's books are among the most popular of all time. And while his lyrical language enticed young children to learn to read, many of his quotes resonate with tweens, teens and adults. These writing prompts on Dr. Seuss quotes are a few of his most quotable lines. When used as writing prompts, they will get your students to view the world with a fresh pair of eyes.

1: *Don't cry because it's over. Smile because it happened.*
Everyone suffers loss in their lives. Pick something that was sad for you (your best friend moved away, you lost the championship game, summer vacation came to an end), and write about why there are still so many reasons you had to smile before it was over. Does remembering the fun stuff make it easier?

2: *Unless someone like you cares an awful lot, nothing is going to get better, it's not.*
When we think about the importance of doing big things, we often think about things like someone caring enough to build a hospital in a place that needs one. But caring can also be about something small, everyday things that help make the world a better place. These are necessary too. Even something like cleaning up the mess you make when you eat at the park makes things better. Imagine a world where no one cared enough to do anything to make the world better? What would the world be like?

3: *You can get help from your teachers, but you are going to have to learn a lot by yourself, sitting alone in your room.*
Why do you think you need to ponder over things quietly to learn something? Write about a time when you had an 'aha' moment when you thought something through and came to a truth or a realization about something. It could be a school work problem or a problem that you solved regarding your friends or family.

4: *A person's a person, no matter how small.*
Dr. Seuss was not talking about a person's physi-

cal size. He could just have easily said "a person's a person, no matter what". He wanted people to accept diversity; whether the person is small or large, Asian or Hispanic, short or tall, thin or fat. Can you think of a time when someone was not treated well because they were "different" from the rest? How did you feel when you witnessed the situation?

5: *The more you read, the more you know. The more you learn, the more places you'll go.*
The word *places* in this quote is not meant to be literal. It doesn't mean if you read a lot, you might get to travel to Spain! The places you'll go is meant to indicate how you can expand your horizons by learning as much as you can. What *places* do you dream of going in your life? How could reading help you to achieve these goals?

6. *Why fit in when you were born to stand out.*
Everyone is unique and special in their own way and we should embrace our individuality. Do you know anyone who very individualistic and does not conform to societal expectations? Write about what makes them unique.

7. *Sometimes the questions are complicated and the answers are simple.*

Do you ever overthink things and make them more complicated than they need to be? Write a story about yourself or someone you know who has this habit.

8. *Be who you are and say what you feel, because those who mind don't matter, and those who matter don't mind.*

Don't be afraid of being yourself. Don't waste your time and energy trying to please people who won't appreciate or accept you for who you are, but rather focus on those who care for you. Can you write an example of when this applied to you or someone you know?

Eleven

Writing Prompts on Ralph Waldo Emerson Quotes

Ralph Waldo Emerson (1803-1882) was an American essayist, lecturer, and poet. He was considered a leader of the Transcendentalist movement, which emphasized the importance of individualism, self-reliance, and intuition. Writing prompts based on his quotations will typically center around the topics of self-expression and self-reliance. Watch your students get their creative juices flowing by using these prompts.

1. *To be yourself in a world that is constantly trying to make you something else is the greatest accomplishment.*
Who has never felt peer pressure in their lives? People pressuring you to do things you didn't really want to do. Did you give in or did you stand your ground and resist? Write an essay detailing

an experience you had with peer pressure and how you handled it and what you've learned from it.

2. *For every minute you are angry you lose sixty seconds of happiness.*
Anger can have a negative impact on your emotional well-being. Write a story about a time you just simply lost your cool. How did you feel afterwards? What could you have done differently?

3. *A great man is always willing to be little.*
What is greatness? Is it being powerful, influential and rich? Or is greatness achieved by being humble, willing to learn, grow and serve others? Take a side and build an argument for it either way.

4. *The only person you are destined to become is the person you decide to be.*
Is our destiny predetermined? Or is it up to us to create and shape our own future?

5. *Do not go where the path may lead, go instead where there is no path and leave a trail.*
This quote encourages people to take the road less traveled and think outside the box. Write a

story about a time you did just that. A time when you took the initiative to try something different and discovered new experiences and opportunities.

6. *Shallow men believe in luck or in circumstance. Strong men believe in cause and effect.*
Is this true in your opinion? Do you feel that your fate is shaped by too many circumstances beyond your control, or are you the main architect of your own destiny?

7. *The greatest glory in living lies not in never falling, but in rising every time we fall.*
True success and greatness in life is not determined by the absence of failure, but by your ability to overcome and learn from those failures. Were you ever deeply disappointed by something you failed at in your life? Write a story about it, and most importantly show how you learned from the painful experience.

Twelve

Writing Prompts on Quotes from Current and Historical Figures

Here is a collection of quotes from some of the most influential figures in history. From the ancient philosophers to modern-day leaders, the quotations of famous people have stood the test of time and continue to be relevant today. Some are well known and some are not. But what they all share in common is the power of exploration, inspiration and thought-provoking ideas. Turn these quotes into writing prompts and challenge your students to reflect on important issues such as leadership, courage, and perseverance, while reflecting on their own lives and values.

1: *No one can make you feel inferior without your consent.*
(Eleanor Roosevelt)
This quote speaks to the power of self-esteem and self-worth. It's a reminder that we have the

power to choose how we react to the words and actions of others. Write an essay on how you would advise a friend who was just victimized by negative and harmful words. What would you do or say to restore their confidence and self-worth?

2: *There is nothing in the world so irresistibly contagious as laughter and good humor.*(Charles Dickens)
Write a story about a day that started out being one of the worst days of your life and ended up being one of the best, thanks to the contagious power of laughter and good humor.

3: *A mind that is stretched by a new experience can never go back to its old dimensions.* (Oliver Wendell Holmes)
This quote speaks to the power of learning and personal growth. Write an essay about three things you wish you had learned earlier in life and why.

4: *The right to swing my fist ends where the other man's nose begins.*
(Oliver Wendell Holmes)
This quote is often used as a metaphor to illustrate the concept of legal limits on individual free-

dom and the importance of balancing individual rights with the rights and welfare of society as a whole. Do you feel that in our country the tolerance towards individual rights is too lenient or too restrictive? Or is the balance about right? Write your opinion and use an example.

5, *The way I see it, if you want the rainbow, you gotta put up with the rain.*
(Dolly Parton)
Life is invariably full of trade-offs. Write about something important in your life that you would love to achieve and the "rain that you would put up with" in order to achieve it.

6: *I have not failed, I've just found 10,000 ways that won't work.*
(Thomas Edison)
In other words, *if at first you don't succeed, try and try again.* Write a story about a time this particularly applied to you. Were you proud that you "never gave up?"

7: *In the middle of every difficulty lies opportunity.*
(Albert Einstein)
Often difficult situations can be viewed as an opportunity to grow and learn, rather than as a set-

back. Write an essay about a difficult experience you once faced and on how you stepped out of you comfort zone to solve it.

8: *A person who never made a mistake never tried anything new.*
(Albert Einstein)
It is essential to take risks and try new things. Write a story about something completely new that you started or did in your life recently. Did you feel a sense of satisfaction taking that first step?

9: *Education is not the learning of facts, but the training of the mind to think.*
(Albert Einstein)
Einstein understood the importance of critical thinking and independent thought in education. Some things need to be contemplated upon rather than learning from facts and figures. Can you think of something you learned, not by rote, but by grappling with a problem and coming up with a solution?

10: *I alone cannot change the world, but I can cast a stone across the waters to create many ripples.*
(Mother Teresa)

Can one person, alone, cast so many ripples as to change something in the world?

11: *I am not afraid of an army of lions led by a sheep; I am afraid of an army of sheep led by a lion.*
(Alexander the Great)
Alexander believed that even a large and powerful army led by a weak or incompetent leader would be less formidable than a smaller and less powerful army led by a strong and capable leader. Do you agree with this statement? How important is a strong leader?

12: *Money is a terrible master but an excellent servant.*
(P.T. Barnum)
Write an essay explaining what you think this quote really means.

13: *The only true wisdom is in knowing you know nothing.*
(Socrates)
Socrates knew that true wisdom comes from being aware of your own ignorance and understanding that there is always more to learn. In truth, we are learning all the time. Write about a

new concept you have learned recently and how it has affected you or made you grow or change.

14: *A lie told often enough becomes the truth.*
(Vladimir Lenin)
Do you agree with this statement? Write about a time that you (or someone you know) told a lie or exaggerated a story so many times that you eventually believed it happened just the way you said, even though you know deep down it isn't so?

15: *You miss 100% of the shots you don't take.*
(Wayne Gretzky)
Have you ever let fear keep you from "taking the shot"? What were you afraid of; embarrassment or failure or something else? Write about it.

16: *Man is least himself when he talks in his own person. Give him a mask, and he will tell you the truth.*
(Oscar Wilde)
This is particularly true in our world today, where behind the mask of anonymity, people feel comfortable revealing their true selves on the internet. Which leads to the question, is it better that we know the deep, dark things people reveal about themselves when they "wear a mask"? Or

should it be required that people identify themselves in online discussions, thereby making conversation more civilized, but less truthful?

17: *A single lie destroys a whole reputation for in-
tegrity.*
(Baltasar Gracian)
Was there ever a time when someone you truly
respected and revered told you a lie that made
you change the way you thought about them? Do
you think you could ever feel the way you did
about them before they told you the lie? Write
about the incident and your opinion about the
person both before and after being lied to.

18: *You can't make an omelette without breaking
eggs.*
(Robert Louis Stevenson)
In order to achieve something, it's often necessary to accept and make sacrifices. Write about
something you recently sacrificed in order to ob-
tain an objective.

19: *When one door of happiness closes, another
opens; but often we look so long at the closed door
that we don't see the open that has opened for us.*
(Helen Keller)

Life has many twists and turns. We all suffer set-backs and disappointments, but we're also presented with unanticipated chances and opportunities when we least expect it. The key is whether you can recognize and act upon them when they present themselves. Write an essay about a time when you took advantage of an unforeseen opportunity that came your way. Or, conversely, a circumstance in your life when you missed out on an excellent one, because you were too preoccupied with the "closed door".

20: *Belief and Knowledge. Knowledge is something which you can use. Belief is something that uses you,* (Idries Shah)
Give a clear cut example of the difference between something you know and something you believe, but can't know for certain. Explain how the difference between the two can cause havoc in the world.

21: *The only thing necessary for the triumph of evil is for good men to do nothing.*
(Edmund Burke)
We can testify to the truth and validity of this quote by just observing the world around us or by studying past world historical events. But let's bring it down to a more personal level. Write a

story about a time you could have avoided some-thing bad or unpleasant from happening by just speaking up, but didn't.

More Free Writing Prompts by Grade Level

If you need more writing prompts at some point, you may want to check ExpositoryWritingPrompts.com. This is my website of free writing prompts.

Here you'll find a fresh supply of free writing prompts for all school ages – from first grade to high school.

These prompts are organized by category. For example, Writing Prompts on Pets and Animals, Science & Inventions, Technology, Careers, Leadership, Environment, Endangered Species, Space & Planets, History, Family, Hobbies, Books, Holidays, Music, Creative Writing Prompts by grade, and many more.

About Linda

I'm an award-winning columnist, author, editor and teacher, who has dedicated a lifetime to the wonderful art of making writing fun. My writings appear in a variety of publications, including *Boys' Life, Christian Home and School, Readers' Digest, Chicken Soup for the Soul,* and *Christian Science Monitor*, as well as in many state standardized testing books, including *Measuring Up to the New York State Learning Standards* and *Measuring Up to the Texas Essential Knowledge and Skills*, among others.

During these wonderful years I've had the pleasure of raising three young boys, who have since grown into three young men, who have given me the beautiful gift of grandparenthood.

If you've enjoyed this book please consider posting a review. I'm always happy to hear your comments and suggestions.

www.ingramcontent.com/pod-product-compliance
Lightning Source LLC
Chambersburg PA
CBHW060353130626
46553CB00003B/1215